Growing fruit and vegetables

1) What do we make a lantern from at Halloween?
2) What makes you cry when you peel it?
3) What is green on the outside and white inside?
4) Do melons grow on a tree or on the ground?

True or false?

5) Pine trees do not lose their needles in winter.

6) Forest rangers have to water the trees every day.

7) Some trees can live for more than 100 years.

8) An oak tree grows from a pine cone.

Bark

Bark

1 2 3 4 5 6 7

Did you know that trees grow one ring inside for each year that they live? If you cut through a tree trunk you can count the rings to see how long the tree lived for.

9) Including the bark, the tree on the left lived for seven years before it was chopped down. How many years did the tree on the right live before it was chopped down? Remember to count the bark too.

Exploring the forest

In the picture above:

1) How many trees can you see?

2) How many foxes are there?

3) How many ducks are there?

4) How many children are in the forest?

Answers: 1 = 16, 2 = 4, 3 = 3, 4 = 12, 5 = true, 6 = false, 7 = true, 8 = false (an oak tree grows from an acorn), 9 = 5 years.

Kitchen invaders

Here are lots of lovely things to eat, but 14 non-edible items have appeared among them. Can you spot them all?

Made for each other

Can you match the numbered items in the box on the left with the pictures in the box on the right? For example, the cyclist, 13, goes with the bicycle, Q.

What's missing?

In each of these pictures something is missing.
Can you spot what it is?

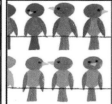

Half of the crocodile is missing. Can you find it?
C

Half of the pig is missing. Can you find it?
E

Half of the fox is missing. Can you find it?
B

Missing pieces

Two children have been to the zoo and taken photos of the animals there. They have made their photos into animal cards. Each card has two parts, but some of the cards have one half missing. Can you find the missing halves from the pictures below?

A

B

C

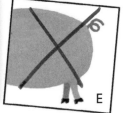

D

E

Half of the penguin is missing. Can you find it?
D

Half of the cow is missing. Can you find it?
A

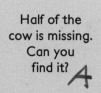

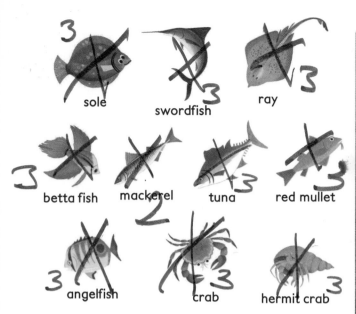

sole   swordfish   ray

betta fish   mackerel   tuna   red mullet

angelfish   crab   hermit crab

Shipwreck under the sea

On the sea bed lies an old wrecked ship.
Divers and sea creatures come to visit it,
looking for treasure or something to eat!
Can you spot each of the creatures above
in the main picture?

Fold in along dotted lines

Woodcutters at work

1) Cut out the picture of the woodcutters and carefully cut along the white piece on each of the capes to make two slits.

2) Carefully fold the picture along the fold lines.

3) Cut around the solid outline of the long strip of arms.

4) Thread the long strip through the two slits you have made in the central section of the card.

5) Pull the strip from side to side to watch your woodcutters at work!

Three in a row

Can you find three of the same picture in a row, either horizontally or vertically, as in the example of these frogs?

At the garage

At this busy garage, cars are repaired, bought, sold and refuelled. The garage staff are running around to keep up with the demand.

Each of these four busy workers appears seven times in the picture. Can you spot them all?

CAR SALES & REPAIRS

NEW CARS

REPAIRS

Outdoor sports

It is a beautiful summer's day and everyone is out playing sports of all kinds. Can you spot...

1) How many blue balls are there?
2) How many dogs are there?
3) How many people are wearing a number?
4) One person is equipped for the wrong season – who is it?

Turn, turn, turn

A merry-go-round goes round and round. Lots of other things turn too. Match the following descriptions to the pictures:

1) My hands turn to show the time. 2) I turn to make a vehicle move. 3) I turn to make holes in a wall. 4) On a hot day, I keep the house cool. 5) I turn in the wind to produce electricity. 6) My light turns to guide ships at sea. 7) The wind turns my sails. 8) I make a car turn corners. 9) I turn to make a speedboat move. 10) I turn in the water to generate power. 11) I turn your clothes to wash them.

Answers: 1 = a clock, 2 = a wheel, 3 = a drill, 4 = a fan, 5 = a wind turbine, 6 = a lighthouse, 7 = a windmill, 8 = a steering wheel, 9 = a propeller, 10 = a water wheel, 11 = a washing machine.

Mommy Squirrel

Squirrel family

Squirrel maze
Mommy Squirrel is trying to get back to her family in the woods. Can you find a way through the trees for her?

House or garden?

Some things belong indoors while others should stay outside. Can you decide if the pictures above should go in either the house or in the garden?

Find the way

Ellie and Sam want to visit their friend Mary. Each time they reach an animal's house they have to change to a different colored path. Can you track their route along the different colored paths to Mary?

Ellie   Sam

Mary

River crossing

Pete and his dog Bess are visiting lots of their animal friends today. The animals live on both sides of a river. To visit all the following animals, in this order, how many times do Pete and Bess need to cross the river?

Starting from the little hut by the river, Pete and Bess visit the three sheep, then Buttercup the horse, followed by Polly the pig, Maisie the cow, Carl the fox, Clarence the goat, Big Bill the bear, Celeste the donkey and, finally, the two hens, Flip and Flap.

Answer: Pete and Bess need to cross the river seven times.

Fun at the zoo

It's always fun to go to the zoo and see all the animals. In this zoo scene, how many penguins, sea lions, pelicans, lions, bears, tigers, snakes and giraffes can you see?

The best route

A duck, a frog, a lizard, a chick and a tortoise all want to visit their friend the fox. However, most of them have a terrible sense of direction and lose their way. Which of them is the only one to reach the fox?

Animals around town

The seven animals shown above have all gone into town but have hit a traffic jam. Can you spot them all in various vehicles?

Which flower am I?

1) My thorns may prick your fingers.
2) My flowers are like little white bells.
3) I have red petals and a black center.
4) I am named after a type of food.
5) My name is one you should remember!

forget-me-not

buttercup

periwinkle

lily-of-the-valley

poppy

daffodil

lavender

marigold

pansy

tulip

mimosa

carnation

iris

aster

cornflower

rose

Forest friends in color

In a clearing in the forest, the animals have gathered together. Some have changed color.

1) How many green foxes are there?
2) How many blue lizards are there?
3) How many pink rabbits are there?

Answers: 1 = 5, 2 = 2, 3 = 3.

At the train station

Can you spot six mistakes in the following description of this scene?

"A freight train has pulled into the station. A female passenger is getting off the train. Five dogs and four birds are watching the people on the platform. There is a boy waving a flag with the number 38 on it and a girl pushing a trolley loaded with bottles."

EXIT

83

Answers: A **passenger** train has pulled in to the station. A **male** passenger is getting off the train. **Six** dogs and **three** birds are watching the people on the platform. There is a boy waving a flag with the number **83** on it and a girl pushing a trolley loaded with **luggage**.

Air or water?

Which of these things would you see in the air?

Which of these animals would live in the water?

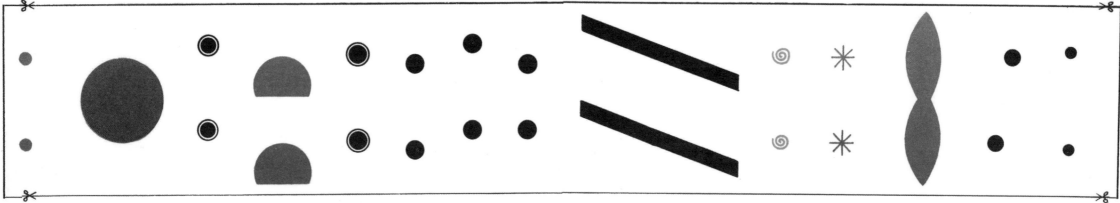

Funny faces

1) Cut around the solid black lines of the four characters above.

2) Carefully cut along the dashed lines at the top and bottom of each one to make two slits.

3) Cut around the solid black lines of the long strip of shapes.

4 Thread the long strip through the top the top slit of one of your characters from the front, then back out through the bottom.

5) Pull the strip up and down to watch your character's eyes change!

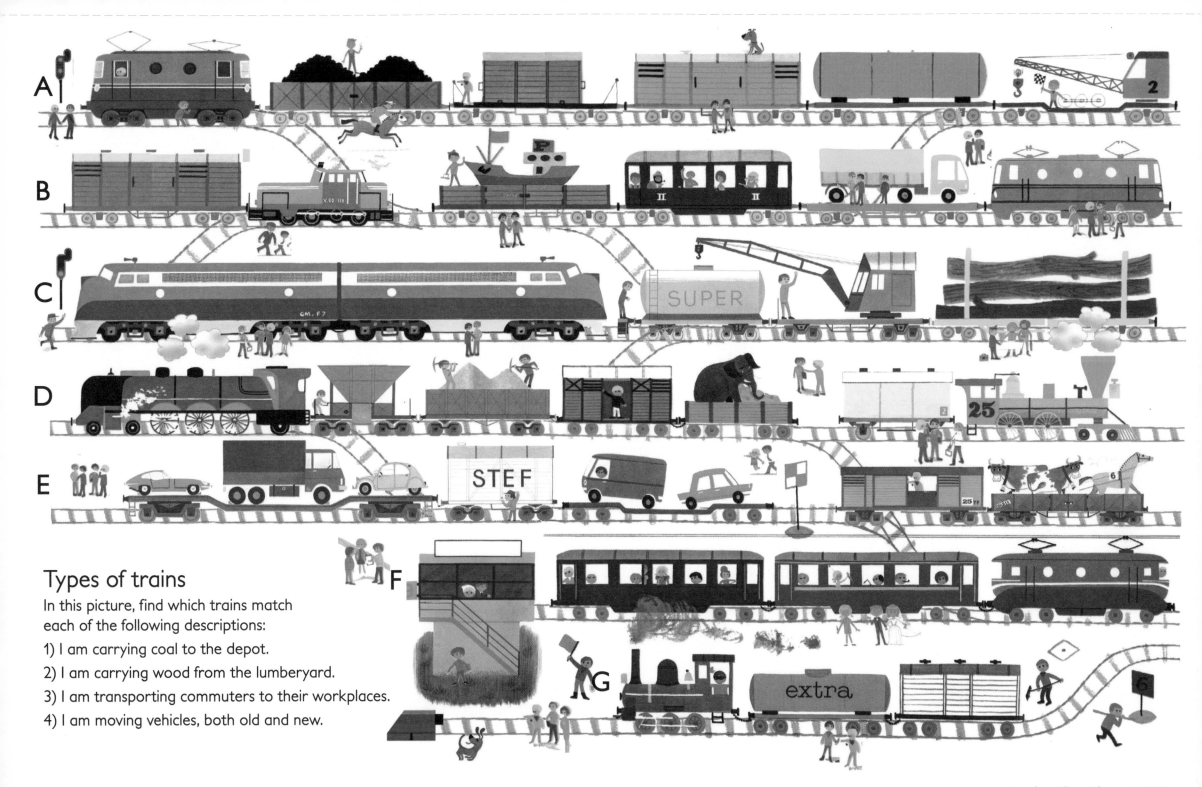

Types of trains

In this picture, find which trains match each of the following descriptions:

1) I am carrying coal to the depot.

2) I am carrying wood from the lumberyard.

3) I am transporting commuters to their workplaces.

4) I am moving vehicles, both old and new.

Jack

Jill

Find the way

Which of these three chains of children
– 1, 2 or 3 – will lead Jack to Jill?

Answer: 3.

Who's on the bus?

All the children pictured below are taking the bus to school. Can you spot them all?

Jack

Olly

Vikram

Nancy

Mike

Ali

Josh

Pilou

Jo

Peter

Hiding in the woods

A number of animals are hidden among the trees in this woodland scene. Can you spot at least ten of them?

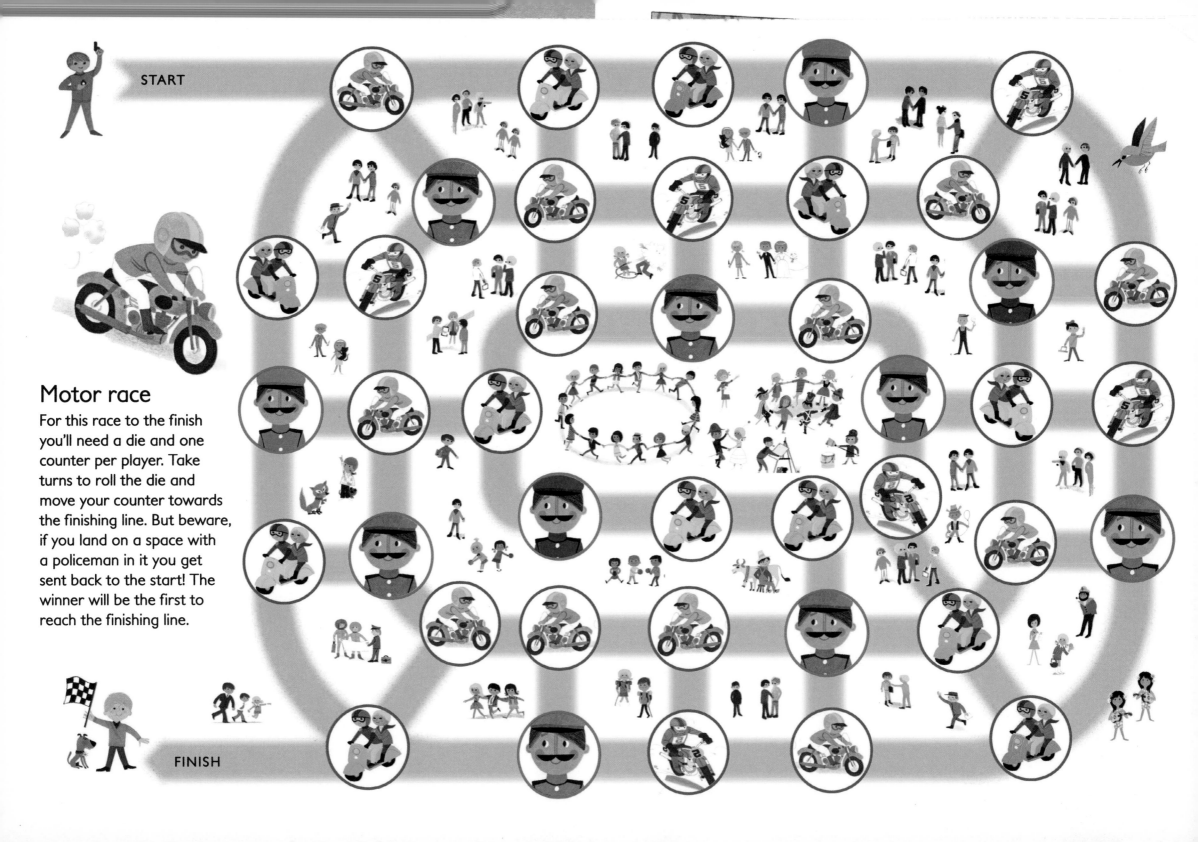

START

Motor race

For this race to the finish you'll need a die and one counter per player. Take turns to roll the die and move your counter towards the finishing line. But beware, if you land on a space with a policeman in it you get sent back to the start! The winner will be the first to reach the finishing line.

FINISH

Romeo's flying lesson didn't go too well! Good job he took his umbrella along…

Romeo's flying lesson

True or false?

1) All airplanes have a propeller.

2) Sea planes can land on and take off from water.

3) Stewards fly the plane.

4) A cargo plane carries only people on board.

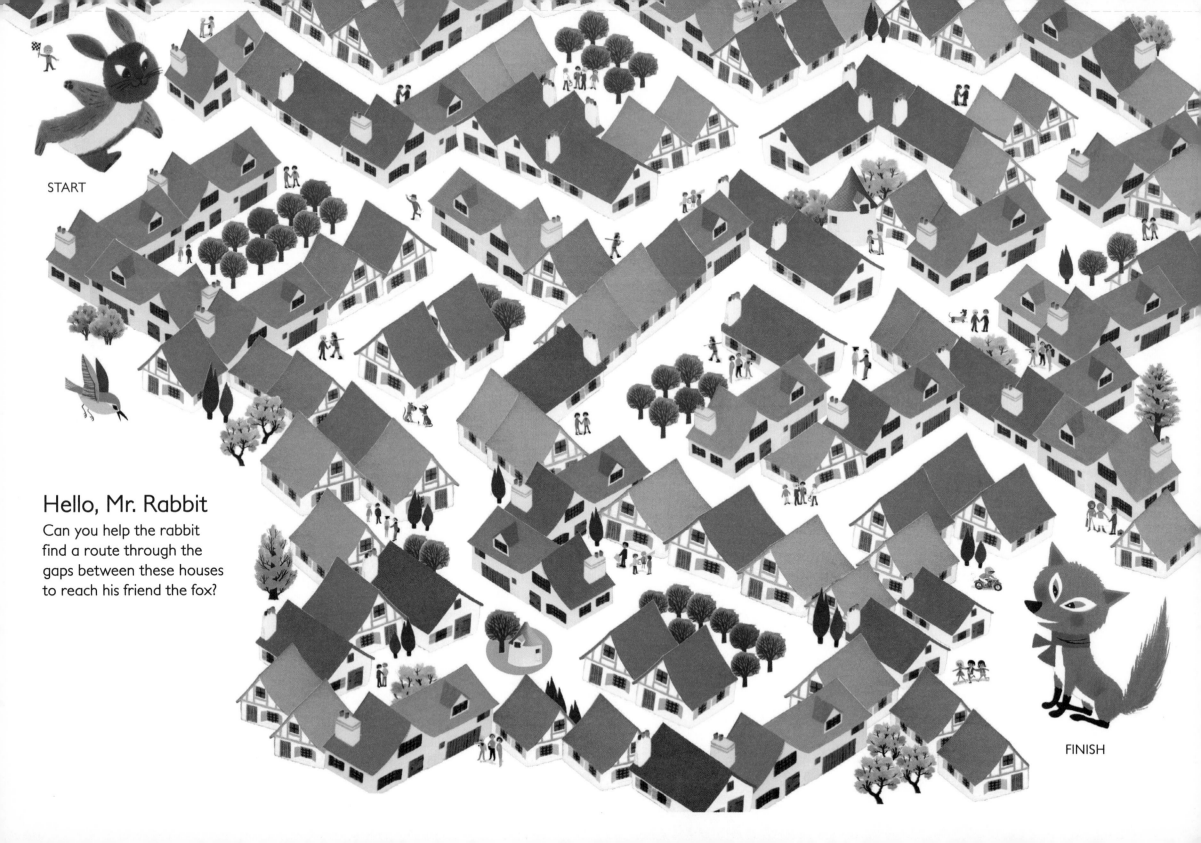

START

Hello, Mr. Rabbit

Can you help the rabbit find a route through the gaps between these houses to reach his friend the fox?

FINISH

Kate

Edie

Lizzie

Mom

Mary

Ben

Upstairs, downstairs

Ben has just got in from school and wants to say hello to everyone. To see all the following people, in this order, how many times does Ben have to go up or down the stairs?

First Ben goes up to his sister Kate's room, then into the kitchen to see his mom. He then stops by the bathroom to say hi to his cousin Lizzie, before going out to see his other sister, Mary, who's watering the garden. Finally, he says hello to his friend Edie, on the landing.

5

Types of truck

In this picture, spot which vehicles match each of the following descriptions:

1) I carry water to put out a fire.

2) I can pull a car that has broken down.

3) I am small but strong enough to lift a crate.

4) I transport new cars to the showroom.

5) I take children to school and back home again.

Up in the air

Can you spot seven differences between these two pictures?

Pictures that don't match

Max and Mary have been out taking photos with their new camera. In each of their four sets of photos there are some small differences – can you spot them all?

A colorful game of volleyball

The player in blue hits the ball over to the boy in green, who passes it to the girl in black, who passes it to the boy in purple, who passes it to the boy in red. He then hits it to the player in yellow, who passes it back to the player in green. How many times did the ball go over the net?

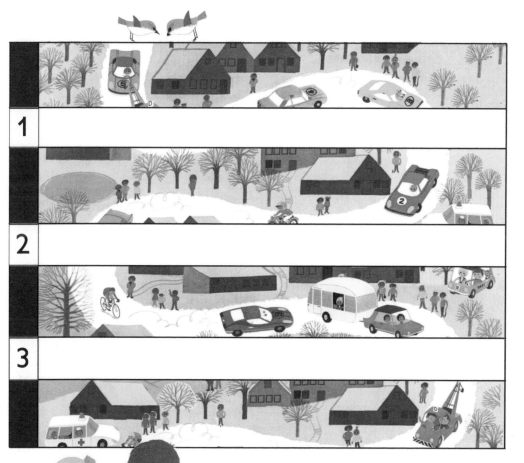

1

2

3

4

5

6

Missing pieces

On this page are a snowy scene and a farm scene with some sections cut out. Can you spot which sections of picture at the bottom of the page go with which numbered spaces on the pictures above?

A

B

C

D

E

F

Crash!

Can you spot five mistakes in the following report of the huge traffic incident pictured?

"Fourteen vehicles were involved in the pile-up, among them a fire truck and an ambulance. The accident occurred when three trucks carrying logs and a green truck carrying a camel spun out of control. Several pigs, dogs and a zebra were among the many passengers who escaped injury."

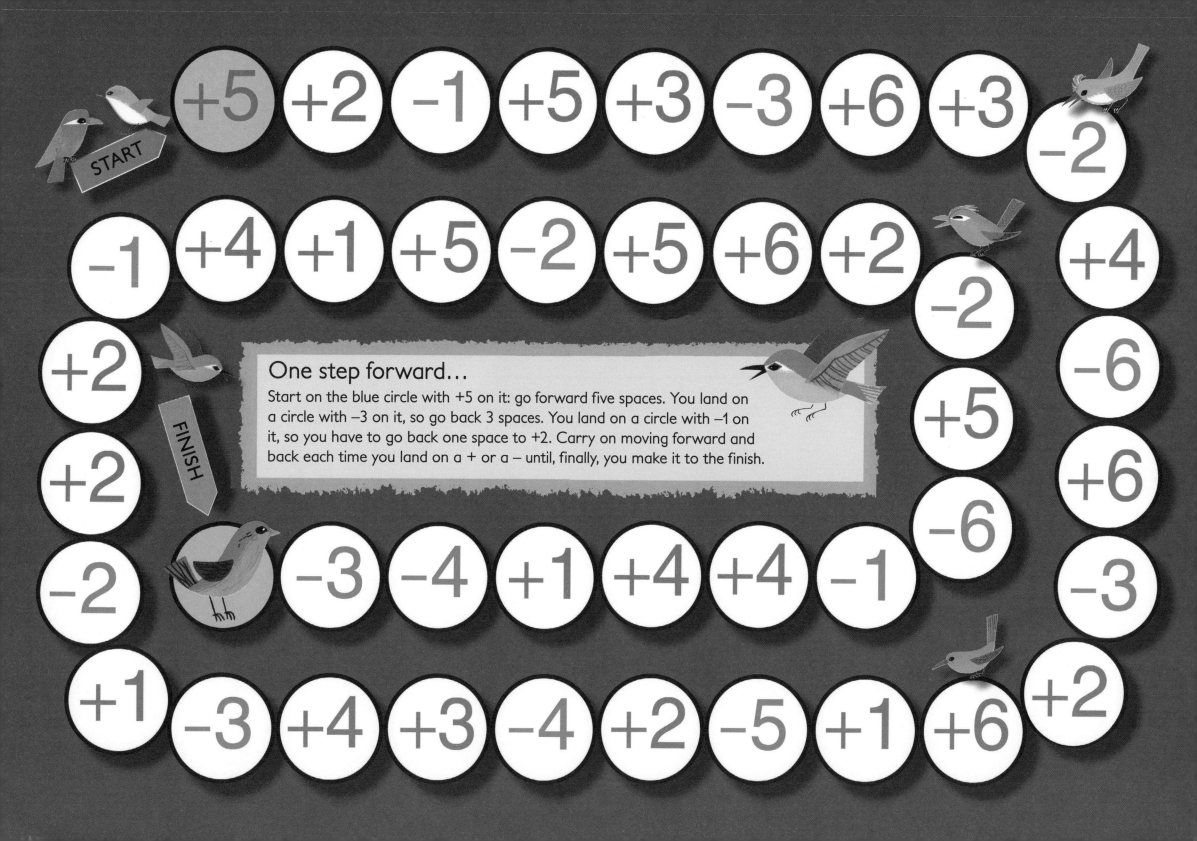

START

+5 +2 −1 +5 +3 −3 +6 +3 −2

−1 +4 +1 +5 −2 +5 +6 +2 +4

−2

+2 −6

One step forward…

Start on the blue circle with +5 on it: go forward five spaces. You land on a circle with −3 on it, so go back 3 spaces. You land on a circle with −1 on it, so you have to go back one space to +2. Carry on moving forward and back each time you land on a + or a − until, finally, you make it to the finish.

+5

FINISH

+2 +6

−6

−2 −3 −4 +1 +4 +4 −1 −3

+1 −3 +4 +3 −4 +2 −5 +1 +6 +2

5

$9 + 14 =$

$20 =$

$9 \times 8 =$

$5 =$

$4 + 4 + 6 + 3 + 2 + 1 = \boxed{26}$

$1 + 16 =$

6

$8 + 8 + 6 + 3 =$

$16 + 9 = \boxed{25}$

Build yourself a house

You will need scissors and glue to build this little house.
Ask an adult for help if you need it.

1) Cut around the black outlines of the five house pieces.
   Start with the walls on this page. You will find the roof,
   chimney and window pieces on the next page.

2) Take the two window pieces and fold the shutters in along
   the dotted lines. Apply glue to the backs of the window
   sections only (not the shutters) and attach the windows
   to the blue spaces on the walls piece.

3) To make an opening door, cut along the two black lines
   on the smaller door and fold along the dotted line.

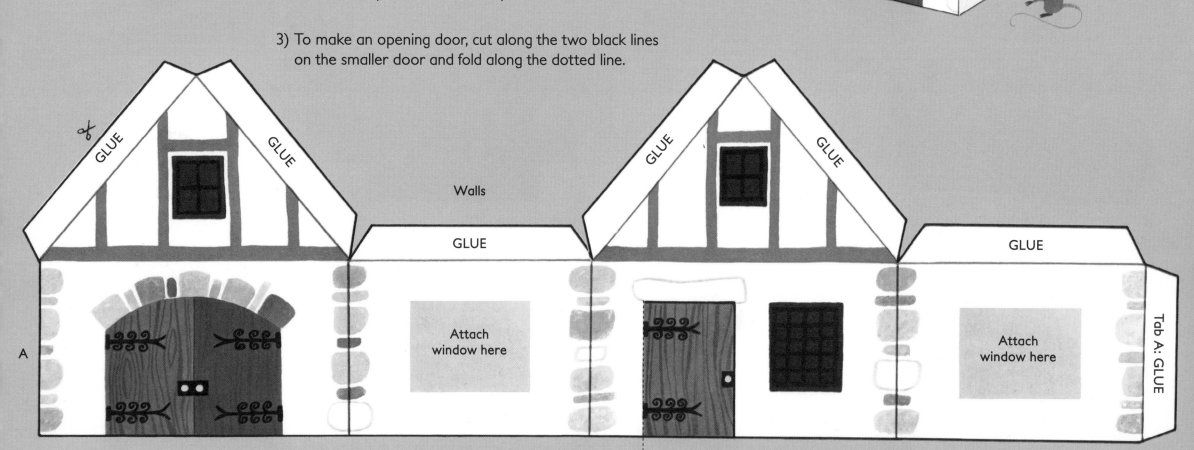

GLUE

GLUE

Walls

GLUE

GLUE

GLUE

GLUE

GLUE

Tab A: GLUE

A

Attach
window here

Attach
window here

Cut along two black lines at top and right side
of door and fold along dotted line on the left

4) Assemble the walls by folding back along all the blue lines. Glue Tab A and stick it to the back of the wall marked A. You will have formed a shape like an open-topped cube.

5) On the chimney piece fold back along all the blue lines. To assemble the chimney, first glue Tab B to the back of the piece marked B. Glue Tab C to the back of the piece marked C. Apply glue to Tab D and stick it to the back of Tab E.

6) Fold the roof piece in half along the dotted line.

7) Apply glue to Tab E on the chimney and attach the chimney to the roof.

8) Apply glue to all six tabs at the top of the walls piece. Carefully place the roof piece on top of the walls to complete your house!

Window

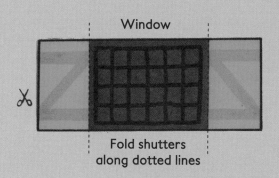

Fold shutters along dotted lines

Window

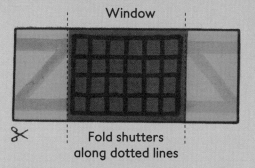

Fold shutters along dotted lines

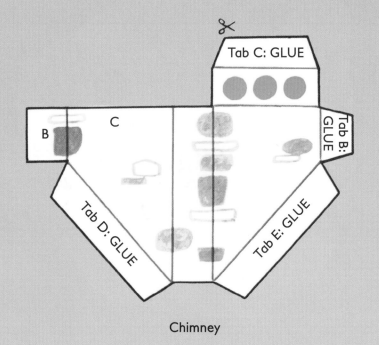

Chimney

Tab C: GLUE

B

C

Tab B: GLUE

Tab D: GLUE

Tab E: GLUE

Roof

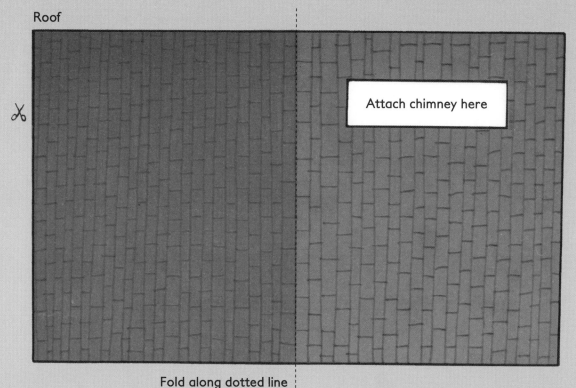

Attach chimney here

Fold along dotted line

Egg heads

Next time you have a boiled egg, keep the shell and use it to make a character with growing green hair.

1) Carefully wash the empty eggshell – don't break it! Draw a little face on your shell as shown, using felt-tip pens.

2) Place a damp cotton ball inside the shell.

3) Gently add some garden cress or grass seeds.

4) Cut out the body piece given here, or you can design and decorate your own using the shape as a guide. Roll it round and glue it in place to form an open-topped cone. Use paper clips to hold it in place while the glue dries.

5) Place your eggshell on top of the cone body as shown below, then place your character on a sunny windowsill. Check every evening that the cotton ball is still damp and add water if it needs it. In a few days your little egg head will have sprouted some funny green hair!

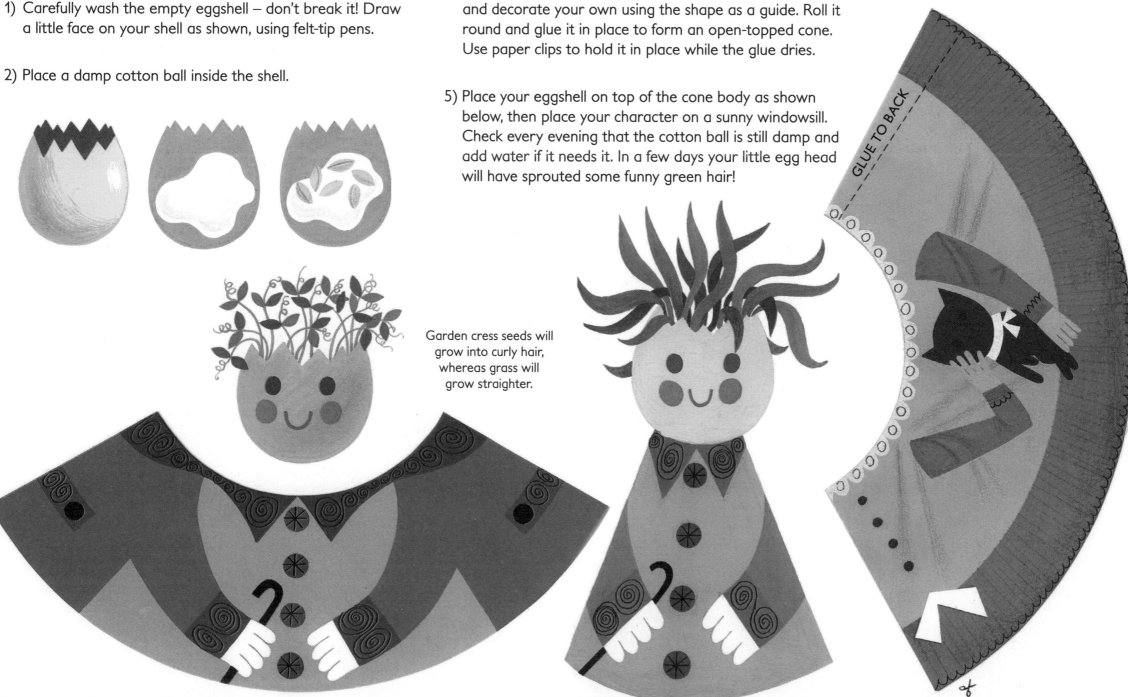

Garden cress seeds will grow into curly hair, whereas grass will grow straighter.

GLUE TO BACK

Make a train

Cut carefully around all the pictures on this page. Mix them up, then see if you can line them up to form one long train.

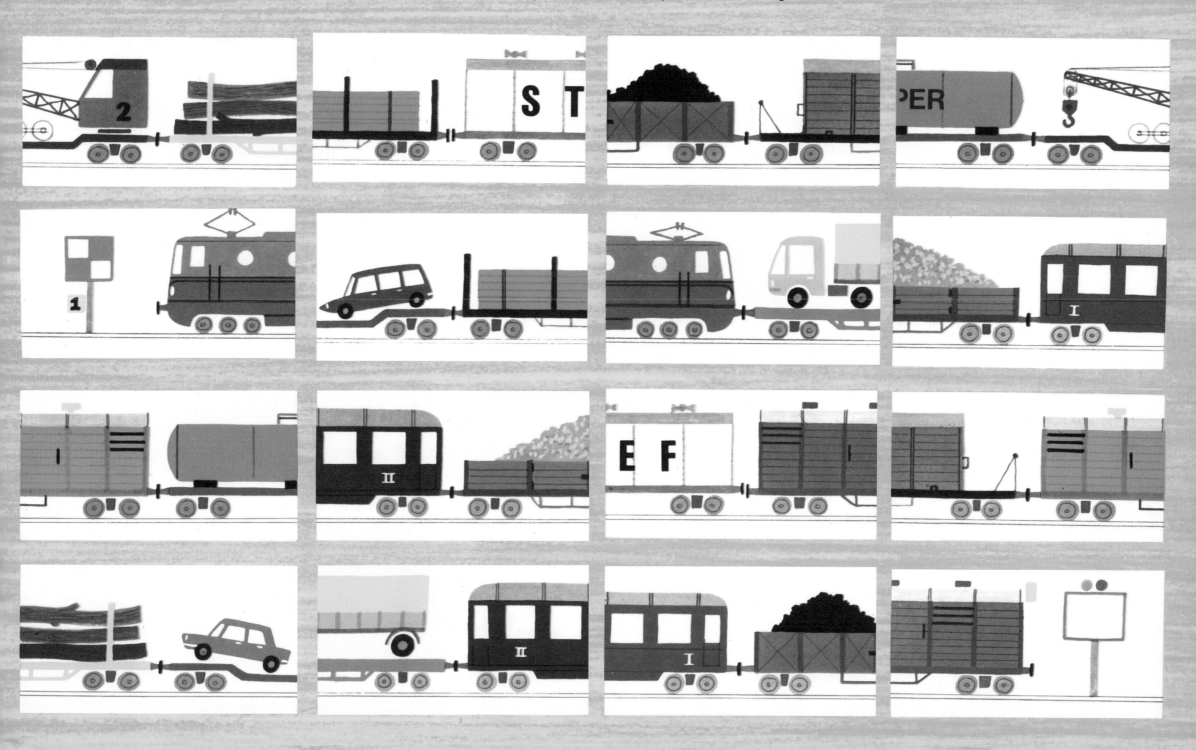

Missing pieces

On this page are a seaside scene and a farm scene with some sections cut out. Can you spot which sections of the pictures at the bottom of the page go with which numbered spaces on the pictures above?

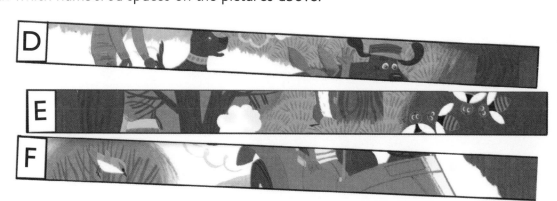

Bees at work

Our friends the bees love to buzz around among the flowers and make honey for us to eat. How much do you know about bees?

1) What do we call the yellow powder that bees collect from flowers? **Pollen**

2) True or false? A bee has four legs and two wings. ~~True~~ **False**

3) What do we call the bee in charge of a hive? **Queen**

4) True or false? Bees can also help us to make candles? ~~False~~ **True**